# Ladybird

Karen Hartley
and
Chris Macro

Heinemann
LIBRARY

First published in Great Britain by Heinemann Library
Halley Court, Jordan Hill, Oxford OX2 8EJ
a division of Reed Educational and Professional Publishing Ltd.
Heinemann is a registered trademark of Reed Educational & Professional Publishing Limited.

OXFORD FLORENCE PRAGUE MADRID ATHENS
MELBOURNE AUCKLAND KUALA LUMPUR SINGAPORE TOKYO
IBADAN NAIROBI KAMPALA JOHANNESBURG GABORONE
PORTSMOUTH NH CHICAGO MEXICO CITY SAO PAULO

Designed by Celia Floyd
Illustrations by Alan Male
Printed in Hong Kong / China

02 01
10 9 8 7 6
ISBN 0 431 01682 8
This title is also available in a hardback library edition (ISBN 0 431 01675 5)

**British Library Cataloguing in Publication Data**

Hartley, Karen
    Ladybirds. - (Bug books)
    1. Ladybugs - Juvenile literature
    I. Title II. Macro, Chris
    595.7'69

**Acknowledgements**
The Publishers would like to thank the following for permissio
Thurston p29; Bruce Coleman Ltd: D Austen p25, W Cheng \
H Reinhard pp4, 19, F Sauer p21, K Taylor pp12, 28; NHPA: S
Scientific Films: P Franklin p16, S Littlewood p15, A MacEwen p20, A Ramage pp10, 11, 26, I Shepherd p22; Premaphotos: K Preston-Mafham pp9, 17, 23, 24; Science Photo Library: J Burgess p7

Cover photograph reproduced with permission of child; Chris Honeywell, ladybird; C Nuridsany & M Peronnou/Science Photo Library

Every effort has been made to contact copyright holders of any material reproduced in this book. Any omissions will be rectified in subsequent printings if notice is given to the Publisher.

Any words appearing in the text in bold, **like this**, are explained in the Glossary.

# Contents

# What are ladybirds?

Ladybirds are **insects**. There are 42 different kinds of ladybird in the United Kingdom. There are hundreds more around the world.

Ladybirds are small **beetles** with a round body like half a ball. They have six legs and two pairs of wings. Most are red or yellow with black spots.

# What do ladybirds look like?

Some ladybirds are black with red spots and some are black or brown with white spots. We are going to look at red ladybirds with black spots.

Ladybirds have two eyes that can see up, down, backwards and forwards all at the same time. They have two **feelers** for touching and two jaws for biting.

# How big are ladybirds?

Some kinds of ladybird are bigger than others. An eyed ladybird, like the one in the picture, is 7 mm long. That is about as long as your little fingernail.

These 16-spot ladybirds are very, very tiny. They are only 2 mm long. They are the same size as the top of a pin!

# How are ladybirds born?

In spring and summer the weather is warm and female ladybirds lay eggs on the underside of leaves. The eggs are **oval** and pale yellow.

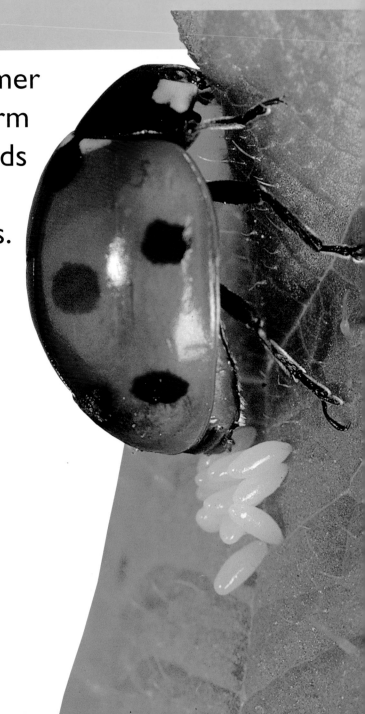

After 4 days a **larva hatches** out of each egg. The larvae are called grubs. Some ladybird larvae have black, pointed bodies and six legs.

# How do ladybirds grow?

When the **larvae hatch**, they grow very quickly and **moult** three times in three weeks. The larvae turn dark blue with yellow or red spots.

After 4 weeks each larva fixes its body to a leaf and turns into a **pupa**. A week later it splits open and out crawls a ladybird. It stretches its wings to dry.

# What do ladybirds eat?

Most ladybirds look for greenfly to eat but some kinds of ladybird eat the leaves of plants.

**Larvae** eat the same food as adult ladybirds. A grub will eat more than 200 greenfly before it turns into a **pupa**.

# Which animals attack ladybirds?

Not many animals attack ladybirds because their bright colour warns that they do not taste nice. Some kinds of spider eat ladybirds.

Sometimes ants attack ladybirds and try to stop them from eating greenfly. The ants want the greenfly for their own food.

# Where do ladybirds live?

Ladybirds live where they can find food to eat. They also need leaves where they can lay their eggs.

You will find ladybirds where there are lots of flowers or trees. They eat the greenfly that live on the leaves or stems of the flowers.

# How do ladybirds move?

Ladybirds use their wings to fly to look for food. When they land on a plant, they fold their wings under their wing-covers.

When a ladybird climbs up a stem it holds on with all of its six feet. It crawls very quickly to catch the greenfly.

# How long do ladybirds live?

Most ladybirds live through the spring, summer and autumn. Many die in the winter because they cannot find enough food to eat.

Ladybirds do not like the cold weather. In the winter you may sometimes see them huddled together on the trunk of a tree or under a big stone.

# What do ladybirds do?

People who have gardens like ladybirds because they eat pests. Pests harm the plants in gardens.

Sometimes farmers bring lots of lady-birds to their farms and **orchards**. The ladybirds eat greenfly and other **insects** that kill the farmer's crops.

# How are ladybirds special?

When a ladybird comes out of its **pupa**, its colour is very pale and it has no spots. It takes about 2 days to become bright red with black spots.

Ladybirds do not have ears so they cannot hear. They can feel **vibrations** with their feet so they know if something is coming.

# Thinking about ladybirds

Do you remember what happens to the ladybird's eggs after she lays them?

How do ladybirds grow?

This child is going to look after some ladybirds. What do you think the ladybirds will need to eat?

# Bug map

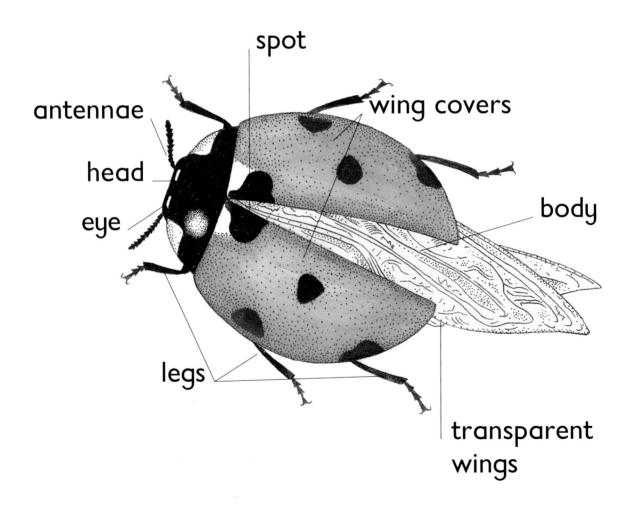

spot

antennae

wing covers

head

eye

body

legs

transparent
wings

# Glossary

**beetle** an insect that has hard wing-covers to protect its wings

**feelers** two long thin tubes that stick out from the head of an insect. They may be used to smell, feel or hear.

**hatch** to come out of the egg

**insect** a small creature with six legs

**larva** (more than one = larvae) the grub that hatches from the egg

**moult** when the larva grows too big for its skin it grows a new one and wriggles out of the old skin

**orchard** a place where lots of fruit trees grow

**oval** a shape that is almost round, like a squashed circle

**pupa** (more than one = pupae) older larva. The adult ladybird grows inside it.

**vibration** the wobble that happens when something moves backwards and forwards very quickly

# Index